The World Eats Butterflies Like You

poetry and prose

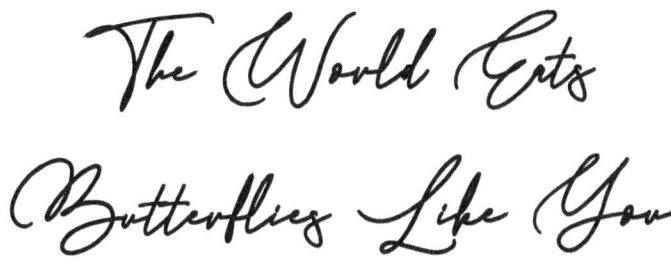

The World Eats Butterflies Like You

Isabelle Quilty

QUERENCIA

Querencia Press, LLC

Chicago, Illinois

QUERENCIA PRESS

© Copyright 2023
Isabelle Quilty

ISBN 978 1 959118 23 7

www.querenciapress.com

First Published in 2023

Querencia Press, LLC
Chicago IL

Printed & Bound in the United States of America

CONTENTS

I dedicate this collection to Peter and Emma. Thank you for always believing in me and encouraging me to follow my passion.

Preface

This collection is for everyone who has ever felt othered in their life. It's for everyone who has ever felt like there is no place for them in a world like this. *The World Eats Butterflies Like You* is a poetry collection written for women and non-binary folk. It's for the queer, plus sized, and everyone who doesn't quite fit in. Growing up, I sought reassurance from the wider world that it was okay for me to exist. Queer, neuro-divergent and plus-sized I always felt like a mistake. Nothing ever matched up, nothing ever felt right. Each poem in this collection is a reminder that we are all deserving of love, freedom and respect. We make our own place in the world, and this is my way of carving out a part for myself.

The Bellflower

The Leaves and Me

The butterfly crawls from my mouth
Finally free
Peacefully into twilight
Find yourself, little friend
Break the chains
Figure all the little things out that I never could
Rest easy
Know that pain doesn't come freely
I could just hold you, yeah?
There's a sour drop of pleasure
Squeezed right onto your tongue
It's alright, alright?
The body you left is hollow, trapped in a space both dark and
precious
Its bones feed the forest floor
The flesh, I saved it for the ants
The marrow will be sweet when you suck it right out
Lick your lips and tell me how delicious the sound of blood clots and
sunken eyes sound
Tell me if it hurts, yeah?
Plagues and cancers
Wars and widows
I'll be right here, the hollow husk beneath the trees and leaves

Hot Pink Blade

Sometimes all the power in the world settles in a blade
Touch me again, I dare you
A crooked grin is shaped with sharp sticks and a breath stinking of alcohol
Red lace runs over her nipple
Are you peaking right now?
You have your own tricks
Strip yourself bare and wait for her to smell the weakness
Cloak her in honey and call her yours
Trust me,
She'll forget about you by morning

Bird Watcher

Here, we drink from the skulls of birds
Shots, really
Acid on the tongue
Heaven down the throat
In this grove of ours
Eat plenty
The fruit is yours to suckle on
The juices are sweet, and the flesh is tender
Let me take you by the tips of your fingers
Skin to skin
Your heartbeat flutters
Our rib cages entwine, and for a fraction of a moment, we are free

All the Secrets in the Sky

Pretty girls have a way of doing hideous things
They can hide soft jealousies well
I can hide tears better
Beneath bedsheets
In the early morning hours
When the world takes a breath
And it's okay to exist
In this place void of time
It's just you and the night sky, little girl
My neck arches back
My nose is cold
Feet sore
But the stars are here with me now
The world lies before me
An infinite invitation
A mirror for a mirror
The universe sighs, the most minute pity
A teardrop of the night descends
And it exists behind my cornea
It will never be taken from me
Until ash becomes me
Or a knife slides into the tender, curious flesh of the eye
And you can all watch the secrets of the universe spill out of my
skull

You can't chase ghosts that don't want you

We live in a world enveloped by specters. They have blue eyes, they crave flesh and wander about in the moonlight. They might ask you something mundane, like, why are you staying up so late? It won't chase the thoughts away forever. You can't keep doom scrolling until your hand cramps and your eyes are dry and bloodshot. They'll find you in the morning anyway. You want to drown that stuff out, I get it. We all get it. Try and get some sleep, it's easier said than done, right? So close your eyes, and think of a forest. You're laying down on the forest floor, the blue sky stretches above, interrupted by a canopy of golden leaves. They rain down in the soft, warm breeze to join you on the floor, forming a bed just for you. Reach a hand out to the cloud that drifts by and let your fingers catch it. The water runs down the palm of your hand, dancing down your wrist. Drink from it and find rest.

The Bellflower

I often wonder if I was made too soft for the world. When I was a kid I sat in the back of my parent's car and learnt to crush and compress every feeling into a tightly knotted ball and hide it deep within. I couldn't hurt if I learnt to swallow every jagged-edged emotion. I got older, things got sharper. Feelings turned to glass. They shattered easily under the glare of the others. I still swallowed them piece by piece and let them cut my insides to ribbons.

In the time between then and now, I have learnt much.

I am ash as I am salt
The ocean becomes me
I am vast within
All the stars in the world are for me to swallow, if I so wish
I am more than a hollow, broken shell
I am air as I am fire
Wrap silk across my eyes and I'll still see the universe
I am gentle
I am kind
And I eat the flesh of hearts
Glass and all

The Night Flowers

Lavender Water

If you could hold a wish within your heart
Would you watch it bleed out between your fingers?
Could you catch the droplets before they made it to the bathwater?
Dip the tips of your fingers on your tongue
Taste that fragrance, baby, I made it just for you
Upturned chin, now face the stars
Stay still and silent while bodies morph against one another
It's just another kind of violence
In the search for kindred hearts amid murky waters
Do you find lands of all kinds come to you when you dip your head
beneath the waters?
I remember plenty when the breath leaves me
Bubbles quake on the surface
The only reminder that I'm here, I'm here, I get to exist, don't I?
The lavender's growing softer now
It's made an armour to kiss your skin
Gently, in the way lovers do
The petals stick to my stretch marks
Tracing the lines all the way to my waist
Gently, in the way lovers do
These petals, orchids, sunflowers, and daisies
Are the gems that line my armour
Just like that, baby
There are fractions of myself I leave behind in mirrors
Shop windows
The camera on my phone
The reflections in bathwater
It will take a while to go back to every one
Take them into the palm of my hand
Crush, crush
Uncurl my fingers, and see it for myself
In the lavender water, I am free from such responsibility

What kind of wolf are you?

Are you the kind that eats girls like me?
No
You like to hang open-mouthed, ready to swallow me whole
Bones and skin and all the delicious flesh
The threat hangs above and below
It has followed me every day since I was eleven years old
The threat
The promise
Know a beast for long enough, and soon you'll crave the idea
The wish to be consumed
From head to foot
The wide, masculine shoulders
Wide hips
Heavy breasts and tired eyes
Roughly cut cuticles
Teeth I grind in my sleep
Find enough of me to break
And soon enough I'll befriend the wolf
I've memorised its fangs
42, to be precise

Butterfly Kingdom

I don't quite fit in these shoes yet
They fall flat on the asphalt
Awkward when I take the steps to and from
I'll learn to keep my head down
Eyes on the ground
Count the cracks in the pavement
Eye contact means they see you
Can't let them past the guard
The wall
The prison
It doesn't work like that here in the butterfly kingdom

Here in the kingdom, the wind in my hair
Sugar sticks to my lips
All decadent
All plain to see
The scars
Stretchmarks
The acne
The simple strength of being me

A Ruptured Falling Star

They find themselves in between leaves
Still soaking, the tea is forming
Their bones tend to creak this early in the morning
Remembering when they would sweat and felt happier for it
It wasn't a protest
To feel good when they wake in the morning
They wish to know the truth of things
Real pain
The real cold
Feel leeches on the skin
The night sky is their cloak, the moon a grandfather's wrinkly smile
Let them tumble through the woods and pave a better road
May it lead them into the icy embrace of the stars
They are glass fractures, beings of indifferent light
They will be welcomed amongst them
With their scarred skin
The red sores on their breasts
The dark rings beneath their eyes
Chapped lips and wide grin
Mischief intertwined with subtle gazes
as blood is stardust made red and earthly
They mutter silent prayers for a wilder spirit
And every night they dream of the wildwood
Thorns and cracked limbs
The spirit is made of patchwork victories over mountain streams
and glaciers of the midnight sky
They dream of the road-worn, hoping to take another step
For greater beginnings
And brighter mornings

The Significance of Sweet Things

Our greatest memories are the ones we can taste. This is where ghosts make their home. In the paper-thin line between scent, memory, and the sweetness of our youth, apparitions nestle. They shuffle in close together, some pouring over one another like phantasmal spilled syrup.

Perhaps my stretch marks have become taut and strained over memories that should live innocently in the recesses of my mind. Maybe years of judgment for every mouthful of food eaten is enough to sour a person. Eating in public becomes a spectacle, *everyone is invited to the show!*

Feminine presenting and fat. Full of sugar and memories, bitter to the taste.

I have decided to make my own space. I press two fingers to my temple, the base of my spine, and the heart of my throat. There is power there. Fire and kindling, earth, and air, all bound up in a body that I believe is as kind as it is fat. I wish to burn and let my skin become ash. I want my smoke to fill the room. I want to let the roar of the flames speak over everyone with a voice you can't ignore.

Night Flowers

Night traces her fingers across my jaw
She finds quiet places such as this
To thrust the hilt of the silver blade into my hands
It's to keep me company as I sleep
An eternal dance
A lifetime I will live steeped in agony and obsidian
With a heart connected by ventricles of stone
My place in the world is stolen
Shifted
And shunted
I am a Night Flower forevermore
With eyes of inky black to see the world
A silver blade dances at my fingertips
And a blanket of stars to keep me warm

Chaos and the Cage

The Goddess in Your Ribcage

A girl can hold all the strength in the world and still find herself
buried beneath it all
We are taught to let rage go
Anger
Pain
Grief
The snarl in her voice
All of this, is reserved for men
Smile, smile
Easy your features
Lax your grip
Let it go
No
Listen to the goddess in your chest
She thrums with power, memory, and the venom on your tongue
Remember her
Remember her
She is you
You are her
United in strength, hatred held close to the chest
Fuck the weakness they push into us from birth
The meek
The doe-eyes
Let your rage crackle and spark
Hot and fierce
Let the kindling grow
Until it has burnt it all down

Ghost Walker

Parasites love hollow places
They see the dark
And call it warmth and comfort
Run your hands down your sides
Curl your fingers inside yourself
Check for those nasty fuckers
They bite deep
The blood dribbles between white teeth
He'll find you at midnight
You left the light on
A signal of your restless heart
A weakness he loves to suffer

Moths settle in black hair
Mottled and ancient
They're attracted to your kindness
Hook a tooth in
Where the flesh is soft and waiting
Tear, tear, tear
Bend until all is broken
Wrench the parts you want free
Watch her crawl along the carpet, weeping
The cord is snapped and she'll never come back
She belongs to the deep dark sea now

Fray the paintings
Some oil, others spinal fluid
Destroy them with your teeth if you must
Ruination is a party for folk like parasites
Ghost Walkers
They'll pass right by you
Through you
Squirming beneath you
Slam a fist into your chest
Raid your ribcage if you must
Never let them settle in the dark places
Little parasite fuckers

Matters of the Black Cocoon

You can smell death on another person
Dry eyes
Stiff hands
Cracked lips
Leave them?
Leave them be
Fuck it
They're stuck anyway
Death becomes them
It holds onto their insides
Festers them
The pockmarks on the skin
The dark is their funeral politeness
A blanket to hide those fuck ugly scars
Connect their skull with the mirror
So the hallucinations can stop
When you see them stand in front of the mirror
Muttering
Purring
Say nothing
Use them, leech
Say nothing
Fuck them
Use them
Swallow them whole
It was always a hallucination, wasn't it?
A bitter figment
Bile at the back of their throat
Arch the spine, sit straight for your picture
Nobody loves the dying
We all adore the dead
Too bad you couldn't quite make it
Too bad you left her in the black cocoon

To Eat the Wolf that Binds You

Parasites plague the soil, a degradation haunts the soul. Crooked spires scratch overcast skies and the bricks bleed ancient filth. Here, the world remembers all of history. Here, you feel the weight of it all. Your own history. Memories drifting in a haze of cigarette smoke, overdue bills, and second-hand clothes. The jagged scar running down your side. Not the pretty, polite kind you see in movies. This one isn't handsome. It's raised, red and ugly. It holds the memories you'd rather bury.

Here, at the heart of the world, you see the misery and the answer.

It comes in a whisper. *Take, take, take.*

What else have you been good at for all your life?

Be the fire that consumes it all. The prison of fur, flesh, and howls. Take it back. Eat the very thing that contains you.

Take, take, take.

Run your tongue across your canines and let the drool hang.

All that haunts the world can become a feast for you if you have the strength to open your jaws

The Serpent at the End of Things

At the end of all things
A serpent waits to swallow it all
Bone by bone
The liquid ash in your throat
The metallic smell in the back of your nose
Hideous growls best kept in the shadows
Its scales will settle pleasantly on the shoulders of the world
And take us all with a single bite

Chaos and the Cage

There's a certain kind of pain that comes with a clenched jaw and unquiet thoughts. It echoes through every part of my body, crawling under the skin like a faint static from a long-forgotten channel.

Every now and then, the static becomes heat and I am subject to the rotting membrane of fractured chaos.

A moth, painted red
Its wings are delicate as the soul
Creatures like these are just begging to be crushed
They're a smear on the palm
Blood caked underneath the fingernails
Black metal is welded over the mouth and there,
Forever
She will remain
Because pain is a temporary barrier
A solace sought only by those who crave the sweetness
Of release

www.ingramcontent.com/pod-product-compliance
Lightning Source LLC
Chambersburg PA
CBHW051003140626
46546CB00017B/2728